# BEWITCHED

# THE GREATEST SONGS OF RODGERS & HART

Chappell & Co., Inc.

Copyright © 1979 by Chappell & Co., Inc.

# Contents

ALL DRESSED UP (Spic And Spanish), 112

BABES IN ARMS, 36

BEWITCHED, 104

DO IT THE HARD WAY, 116

EV'RY SUNDAY AFTERNOON, 93

EV'RYTHING I'VE GOT, 124

FALLING IN LOVE WITH LOVE, 86

FROM ANOTHER WORLD, 89

GLAD TO BE UNHAPPY, 8

HAVE YOU MET MISS JONES?, 56

THE HEART IS QUICKER THAN THE EYE, 10

I COULD WRITE A BOOK, 108

I DIDN'T KNOW WHAT TIME IT WAS, 16

I WISH I WERE IN LOVE AGAIN, 40

I'D RATHER BE RIGHT, 64

IT NEVER ENTERED MY MIND, 97

IT'S GOT TO BE LOVE, 26

JOHNNY ONE NOTE, 48

THE LADY IS A TRAMP, 29

MY FUNNY VALENTINE, 32

ON YOUR TOES, 12

QUIET NIGHT, 20

THE SHORTEST DAY OF THE YEAR, 78

SIMPATICA, 118

TAKE AND TAKE AND TAKE, 60

THERE'S A SMALL HOTEL, 4

THIS CAN'T BE LOVE, 68

TOO GOOD FOR THE AVERAGE MAN, 22

WAIT TILL YOU SEE HER, 122

WHEN YOU'RE DANCING THE WALTZ, 101

WHERE OR WHEN, 44

WHO ARE YOU?, 82

YOU HAVE CAST YOUR SHADOW ON THE SEA, 70

YOU MUSTN'T KICK IT AROUND, 114

For all works contained herein:
International Copyright Secured
ALL RIGHTS RESERVED     Printed in U.S.A.
Unauthorized copying, arranging, adapting, recording
or public performance is an infringement of copyright.
Infringers are liable under the law.

# THERE'S A SMALL HOTEL

Lyrics by LORENZ HART

Music by RICHARD RODGERS

Copyright © 1936 by Chappell & Co., Inc.
Copyright Renewed

# GLAD TO BE UNHAPPY

*Lyrics by LORENZ HART*

*Music by RICHARD RODGERS*

Copyright © 1936 by Chappell & Co., Inc.
Copyright Renewed

# THE HEART IS QUICKER THAN THE EYE

Lyrics by LORENZ HART
Music by RICHARD RODGERS

Copyright © 1936 by Chappell & Co., Inc.
Copyright Renewed

# ON YOUR TOES

*Lyrics by* LORENZ HART  
*Music by* RICHARD RODGERS

Re-mem-ber the youth 'mid snow and ice,— Who bore the ban-ner with the strange de-vice: "Ex - cel - si - or."___ This mot-to ap-plies to those who dwell___ in Rich-mond Hill or New Ro-chelle, in

Copyright © 1936 by Chappell & Co., Inc.
Copyright Renewed

# I DIDN'T KNOW WHAT TIME IT WAS

Words by LORENZ HART  
Music by RICHARD RODGERS

Once I was young, yes-ter-day, per-haps, Danced with Jim and Paul And kissed some oth-er chaps.

Once I was young, but nev-er was na-ive, I thought I had a trick or two up

Copyright © 1939 by Chappell & Co. Inc.  
Copyright Renewed

# TOO GOOD FOR THE AVERAGE MAN

Lyrics by LORENZ HART  
Music by RICHARD RODGERS

When Rus-sia was white It was white for the class-es And black for the mass-es, Un-for-tun-ate ass-es! All wealth be-longed to few. When Eng-land was Tu-dor, The King and his cron-ies Had cock-tails at Ton-y's, The

Copyright © 1936 by Chappell & Co., Inc.  
Copyright Renewed

# THE LADY IS A TRAMP

*Lyrics by* LORENZ HART

*Music by* RICHARD RODGERS

I get too hungry For dinner at eight,

I like the theatre but never come late.

I never bother with people I hate,

That's why the lady is a tramp.

Copyright © 1937 by Chappell & Co., Inc.
Copyright Renewed

# MY FUNNY VALENTINE

Lyrics by LORENZ HART

Music by RICHARD RODGERS

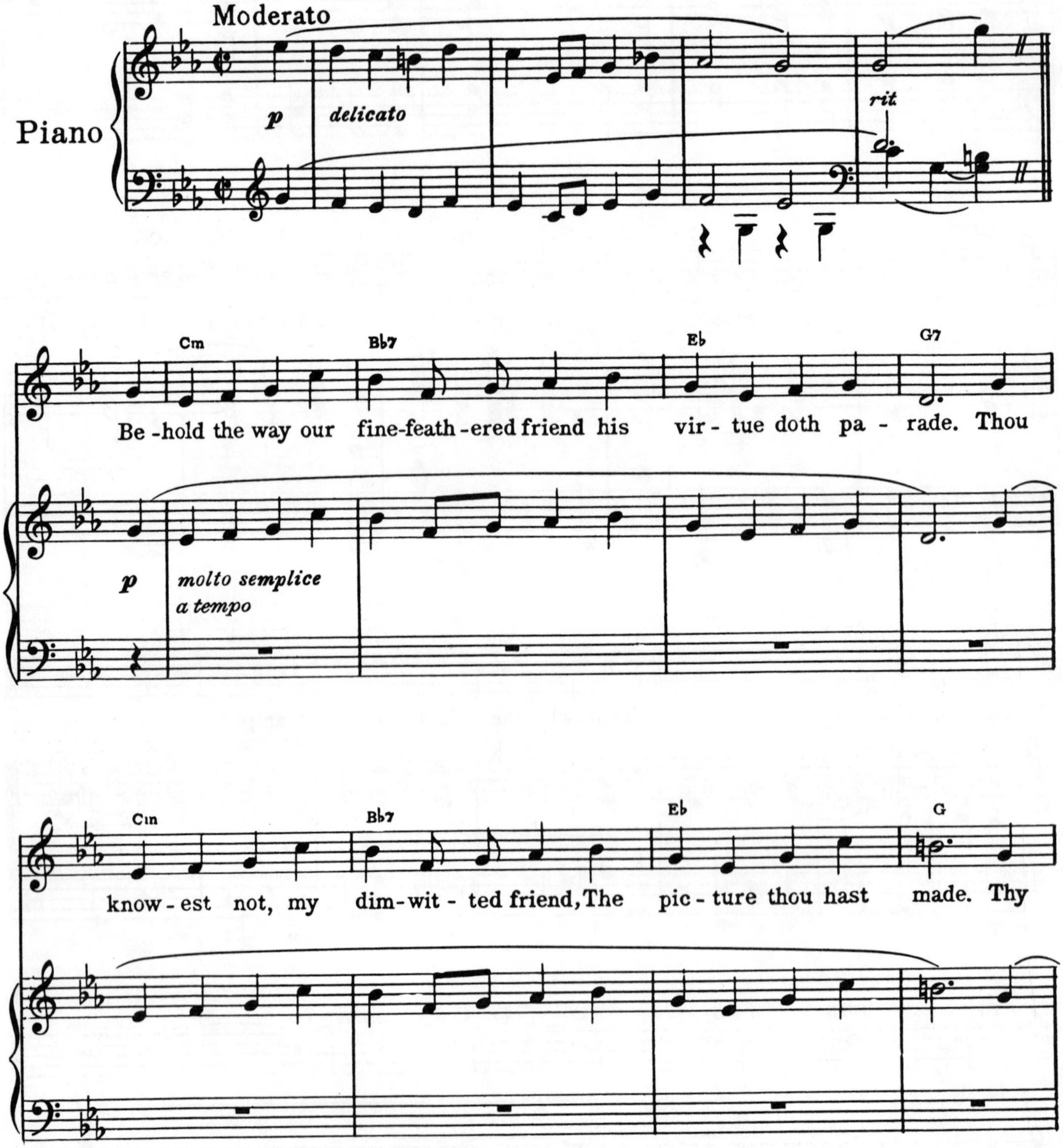

Be-hold the way our fine-feath-ered friend his vir-tue doth pa-rade. Thou know-est not, my dim-wit-ted friend, The pic-ture thou hast made. Thy

Copyright © 1937 by Chappell & Co., Inc.
Copyright Renewed

# BABES IN ARMS

*Lyrics by* LORENZ HART  
*Music by* RICHARD RODGERS

Copyright © 1937 by Chappell & Co., Inc.
Copyright Renewed

Ami.7 Edim. G7 Edim.
Babes in arms, But we'll be laugh - ing
G7 C sempre poco Ami.7
far more. On ci - ty streets and farms
sempre poco
Edim. a G7 poco Edim. G7 crescendo F♯dim.
They'll hear a ris - ing war cry.
a poco crescendo
C mf cresc. molto Dmi.7 F♯dim. C Ami.
Youth will ar - rive, Let them know you're a - live, make it your
mf cresc. molto f

cry___ They call us Babes in arms, They think they must di-rect us. But if we're Babes in arms We'll make them all re-spect us. Why have we

poco
Ami.7
Edim
G7
poco
Edim.
got our arms,
What have we got our
poco
a
poco
G7
cresc.
F♯dim.
C
cresc. molto
Dmi.7
F♯dim.
mf
sight for?
Play - day is done, We've a place in the
mf
cresc.
cresc. molto
C
f Ami.
G7
sun We must fight
for
f
C
f
Ami.
Dmi.7
1.
C
D7
G7
2.
C
So Babes in arms to arms.
arms.
3
f
8va.

# I WISH I WERE IN LOVE AGAIN

*Lyrics by* LORENZ HART
*Music by* RICHARD RODGERS

Moderato

You don't know that I felt good When we up and part-ed.

You don't know I knocked on wood, Glad-ly brok-en heart-ed.

Copyright © 1937 by Chappell & Co., Inc.
Copyright Renewed

Wor-ry-ing is through, I sleep all night,— Ap-pe-tite and health re-stored.

You don't know how much I'm bored!

**Refrain**
1. The sleep-less nights, The dai-ly fights, The quick to-bog-gan when you
2. (The) fur-tive sigh, The black-ened eye, The words "I'll love you till the

reach the heights; I miss the kiss-es and I miss the bites, I
day I die," The self-de-cep-tion that be-lieves the lie, I

wish I were in love a-gain! — The brok-en dates, The end-less waits, The
wish I were in love a-gain! — When love con-geals It soon re-veals The

love-ly lov-ing and the hate-ful hates, The con-ver-sa-tion with the
faint a-rom-a of per-form-ing seals, The dou-ble cross-ing of a

fly-ing plates, I wish I were in love a-gain!
pair of heels I wish I were in love a-gain!

No — more pain, No — more strain,
No — more care, No — de - spair.

Now I'm sane, but I would rather be ga-ga! The pulled out fur of cat and cur, The fine mis-mat-ing of a him and her, I've learned my les-son, but I wish I were in love a-gain! The

I'm all there now, But I'd rath-er be punch-drunk! Be-lieve me sir, I much pre-fer The clas-sic bat-tle of a him and her, I don't like qui-et and I wish I were in love a-gain!

# WHERE OR WHEN

*Lyrics by* LORENZ HART

*Music by* RICHARD RODGERS

When you're a-wake The things you think come from the dreams you dream. Thought has wings, And lots of things are sel-dom what they seem. Some-times you think you've

Copyright © 1937 by Chappell & Co., Inc.
Copyright Renewed

lived be-fore All that you live to-day. Things you do ____ come back to you, ____ As though they knew the way. Oh, the tricks your mind can play!

**Refrain** *(with tender expression)*

It seems we stood and talked like this be-fore. We looked at each oth-er in the same way then, But I can't re-mem-ber where or

E♭maj.7 E♭6 A♭m6 B♭7 E♭ E♭6
when. The clothes you're wear - ing are the
E♭maj.7 Fm7
clothes you wore. The smile you are smil - ing you were smil - ing then,
E♭maj.7 E♭6 Fm6 G7
But I can't re - mem - ber where or when.
Cm Fm7 G7(sus.4) G7 F G7 Cm
Some things that hap - pen for the first time, Seem to be
mp

hap-pen-ing a-gain. And so it seems that we have met be-fore, and laughed be-fore, and loved be-fore, But who knows where or when! when!

# JOHNNY ONE NOTE

*Lyrics by* LORENZ HART

*Music by* RICHARD RODGERS

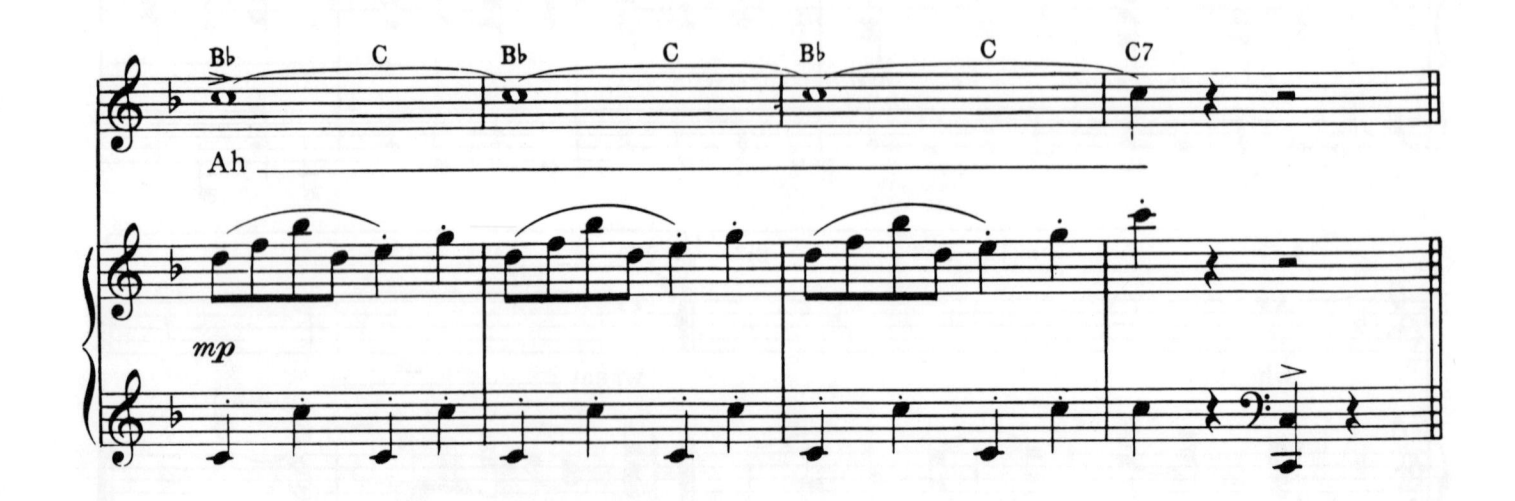

John-ny could on-ly sing one note And the note he sang was this: Ah

Copyright © 1937 by Chappell & Co., Inc.
Copyright Renewed

Refrain brightly
F Eb C7 F C7
Poor John-ny One-Note_ Sang out_ with gus-to_ And
F C7 F Am Gm7 C7
just o-ver-lord-ed_ the place.
F Eb C7 F C7
Poor John-ny One-Note_ Yelled wil-ly-nil-ly,_ Un-
F C7 D7 Gm7
til he_ was blue in_ the face, For

holding one note was his ace. Couldn't hear the brass, Couldn't hear the drum, He was in a class By himself, by gum! Poor Johnny One-Note Got in Aida, Indeed a great chance to be brave.

He took his one note, Howled like the North Wind, Brought

forth wind that made crit-ics rave, While

Ver-di turned round in his grave! Could-n't hear the

flute_____ or the big trom-bone.___ Ev-'ry-one was

mute,_____ John-ny stood a - lone.

**Trio**
Cats and dogs stopped yap-ping, Li-ons in the zoo all_ were

jeal-ous_ of John-ny's_ big trill._____

Thun-der-claps stopped clap-ping, Traf-fic ceased its roar, and they tell us Ni-ag-'ra stood still. He stopped the train-whis-tles, Boat-whis-tles, Steam-whis-tles, Cop-whis-tles; All whis-tles bowed to his skill.

Sing John-ny One-Note, Sing out with gus-to And just o-ver-whelm all the crowd. Ah!

D7 Gm7 F Gm7 C7
So sing, John - ny One - Note, out
F Gm7 C7 F Gm7 C7
loud! Sing, John - ny One - Note!
F Gm7 C7 F crescendo
Sing, John - ny
crescendo
Gm C7 e rit F
One - Note, out loud!
e rit
f marcato

# HAVE YOU MET MISS JONES?

Lyrics by LORENZ HART

Music by RICHARD RODGERS

It happened, I felt it happen. I was awake, I wasn't blind. I didn't think, I felt it happen. Now I be-

Copyright © 1937 by Chappell & Co., Inc.
Copyright Renewed

lieve in mat-ter ov-er mind. And now, you see, we must-n't wait. The near-est mo-ment that we mar-ry is too late!

**Refrain**
*Gracefully and not fast*

"Have you met Miss Jones?" Some one said as we shook hands. She was just Miss Jones to

Gm C7 Gm7 C7 C7+(♭9) F F♯dim
me. Then I said, "Miss Jones,
Gm7 C7 Gm7 C7 Gm7 C7(F) C7 C6 Dm7 C Dm7 G7
You're a girl who un - der - stands, I'm a man who must be
Gm7 C7 F9 E7 Dm B♭ D♭7
free." And all at once I lost my breath, And all at
mf
G♭ A7 D
once was scared to death, And all at once I owned the

earth and sky! Now I've met Miss Jones, And we'll keep on meet-ing till we die, Miss Jones and I.

# TAKE AND TAKE AND TAKE

*Lyrics by LORENZ HART*  
*Music by RICHARD RODGERS*

When a man meets a man on a train— He doesn't talk of crops and rain. When a man sees a mu-sic-al show— He likes the first or sec-ond row. And the man on the train who won't speak of the rain And the

Copyright © 1937 by Chappell & Co., Inc.
Copyright Renewed

man at the show in the ver-y first row, No mat-ter what place they're in Are broth-ers un-der the skin.

You take your brains, You take your gold, I'll take my Beaut-y and take and take and take!

While I take pains not to grow old, I'll take my beauty and make and make and make Beware, rich girls, smart girls, Beware of a fancy rag, A shapely bone, A love-ly hank, o' hair. I can't sew a stitch, can't bake a cake, But watch this cu-ty, Take the cake for beau-ty, Take and take and take! take!

# I'D RATHER BE RIGHT

*Lyrics by* LORENZ HART  
*Music by* RICHARD RODGERS

He: When I first got my job they paid me seventeen a week; In just five years I'm getting twenty-two. I'll get another two buck raise When I've the nerve to

Copyright © 1937 by Chappell & Co., Inc.  
Copyright Renewed

D7 G C6 A7 B7 sus4 B7
speak. She: And if you don't I'll still love you.
A6 B7 mf E7 G D6
You're al-ways right no mat-ter what you do.
mf
Refrain not fast
D D D maj7 Bm D G6 A7
p-mf
I'd rath-er be right than in-flu-en-tial,
p-mf
G6 A7 G6 A7 G6 A7
I'd rath-er be right than wealth-y and

wise, I don't come through, dear, where brains be-long. But per-tain-ing to you, dear, I can't go wrong. I'd rath-er be right than pres-i-den-tial,

Let oth-er folks fight for heights a-bove, What do I fight for? Just to be right for I'd rath-er be right, Just right a-bout love! I'd rath-er be love!

# THIS CAN'T BE LOVE

*Lyrics by* LORENZ HART
*Music by* RICHARD RODGERS

This can't be love be-cause I feel so well,— No sobs, no sor-rows, no sighs;— This can't be love, I get no diz-zy spell.— My head is not— in the skies,— My heart does not stand still,— Just hear it

Copyright © 1938 by Chappell & Co., Inc.
Copyright Renewed

Em7 B7+ E7+(♭9)
beat! This is too sweet to
A9 D7(♭9) D7 G
be love. This can't be love be - cause I
p
C7 G6 Gdim Am7 D7
feel so well; But still I love to look in your
1. G Am7 D7
eyes.
mf
2. G C7 Am7 G
eyes.
mf sf

# YOU HAVE CAST YOUR SHADOW ON THE SEA

*Lyrics by* LORENZ HART
*Music by* RICHARD RODGERS

*(slowly, with expression)*

You have cast your shad-ow on the sea, _____ On
You will cast your shad-ow from the sea, _____ On

both the sea and me. _____ Not a shad-ow
both the land and me. _____ Not a shad-ow

danc-ing in the sun _____ That fades when day is
danc-ing in the sun _____ That fades when day is

done. _____ Since you have made This ten-der
done. _____ Since you have made This ten-der

Copyright © 1938 by Chappell & Co., Inc.
Copyright Renewed

shade for my heart, My heart's no long - er
shade for my heart, My heart's no long - er

free. When you cast your shad - ow on the
free. When you cast your shad - ow from the

sea You'll be with
sea You'll be with

1. me!
2. me!

**RICHARD RODGERS**

**LORENZ HART**

THE BOYS FROM SYRACUSE  THEY MET IN ARGENTINA

BABES IN ARMS

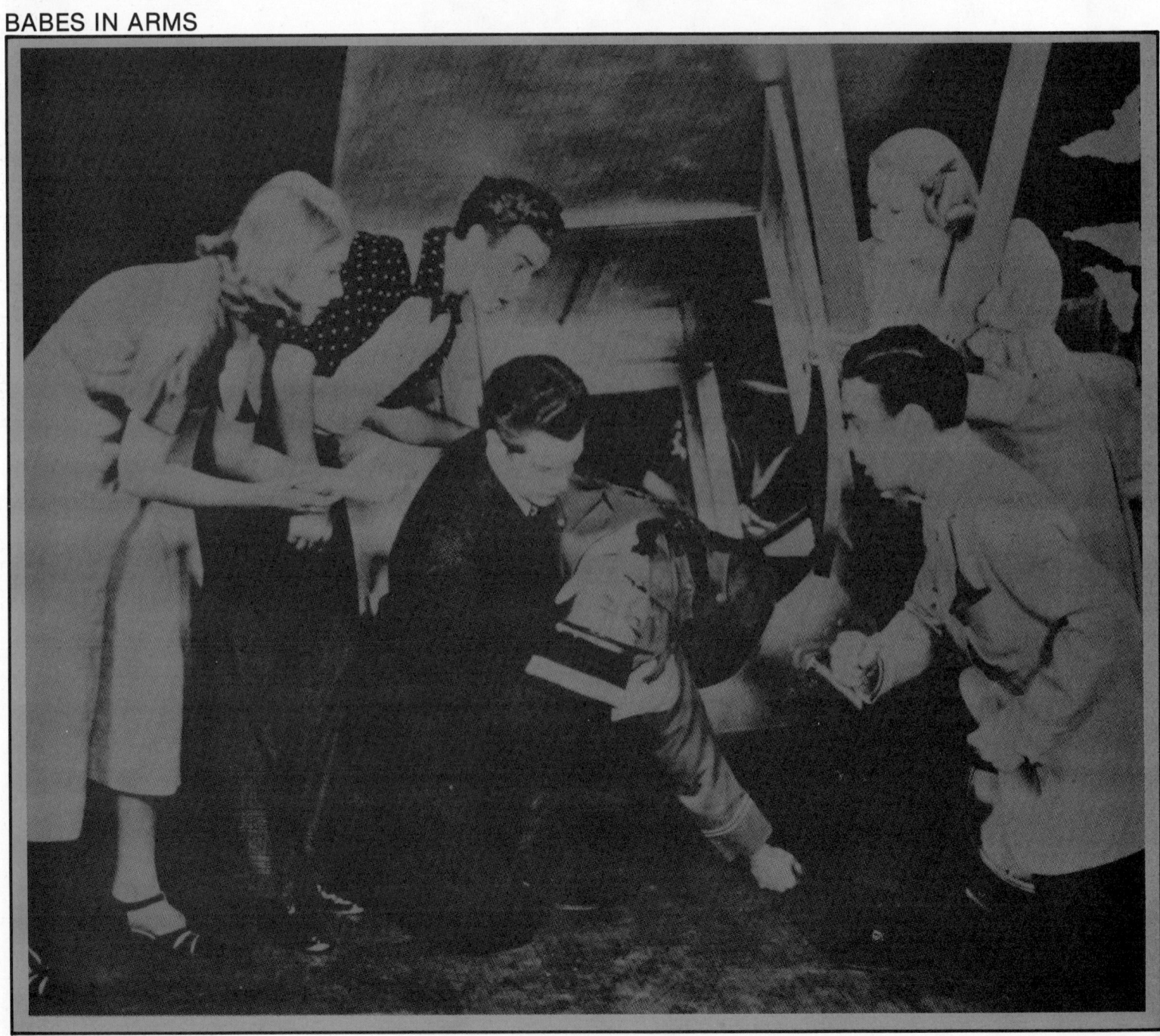

ON YOUR TOES

HIGHER AND HIGHER                    PAL JOEY

LARRY HART & DICK RODGERS AT WORK

RICHARD RODGERS TODAY

# THE SHORTEST DAY OF THE YEAR

*Lyrics by* LORENZ HART  
*Music by* RICHARD RODGERS

It rained the day be-fore we met, Then came three days that I for-get And then, my love, we met a-gain And I re-mem-ber things from then. I measure time By what we do, And so my Calendar is you.

The shortest day of the year Has the longest night of the year; And the longest night is the shortest night with you. The small-est smile on your face Is the great-est kind of em-brace. And a sin-gle kiss is a thou-sand dreams come true. Your soft-est sigh that is my strong-est tie. There's you, there's

I, what can time do? The shortest day of the year Has the longest night of the year, And the longest night is the shortest night with you! The you!

# WHO ARE YOU?

*Lyrics by* LORENZ HART

*Music by* RICHARD RODGERS

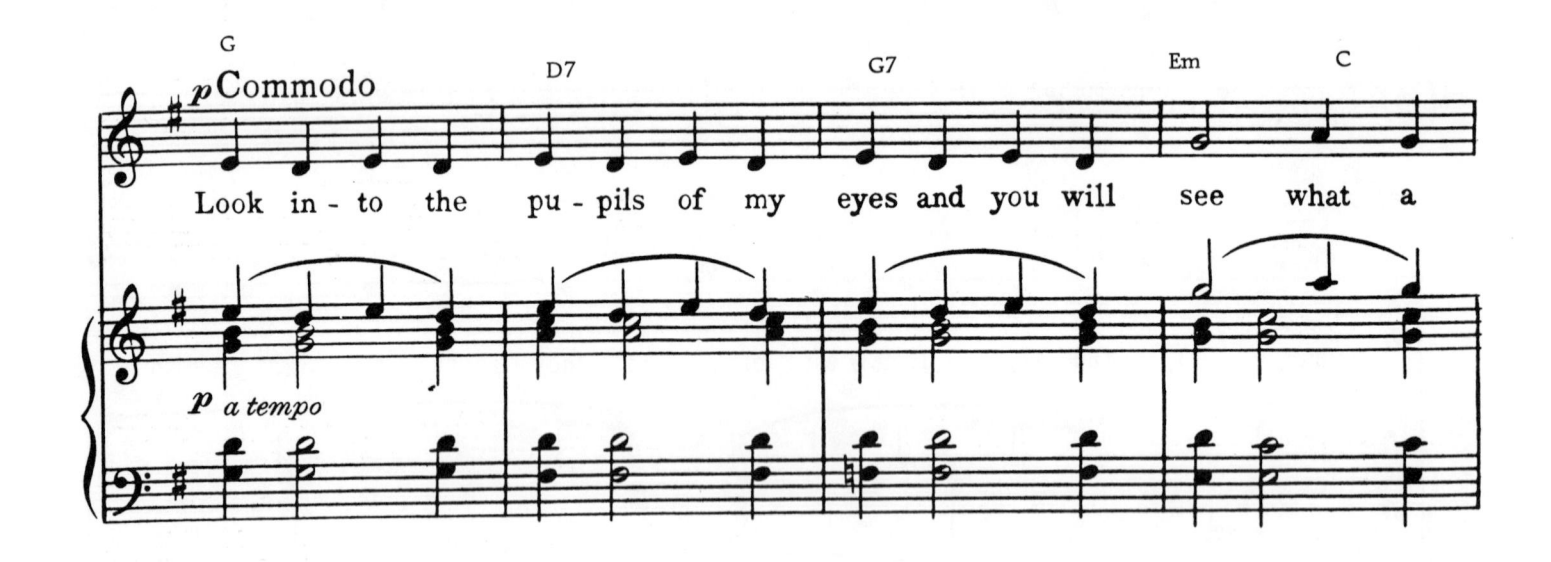

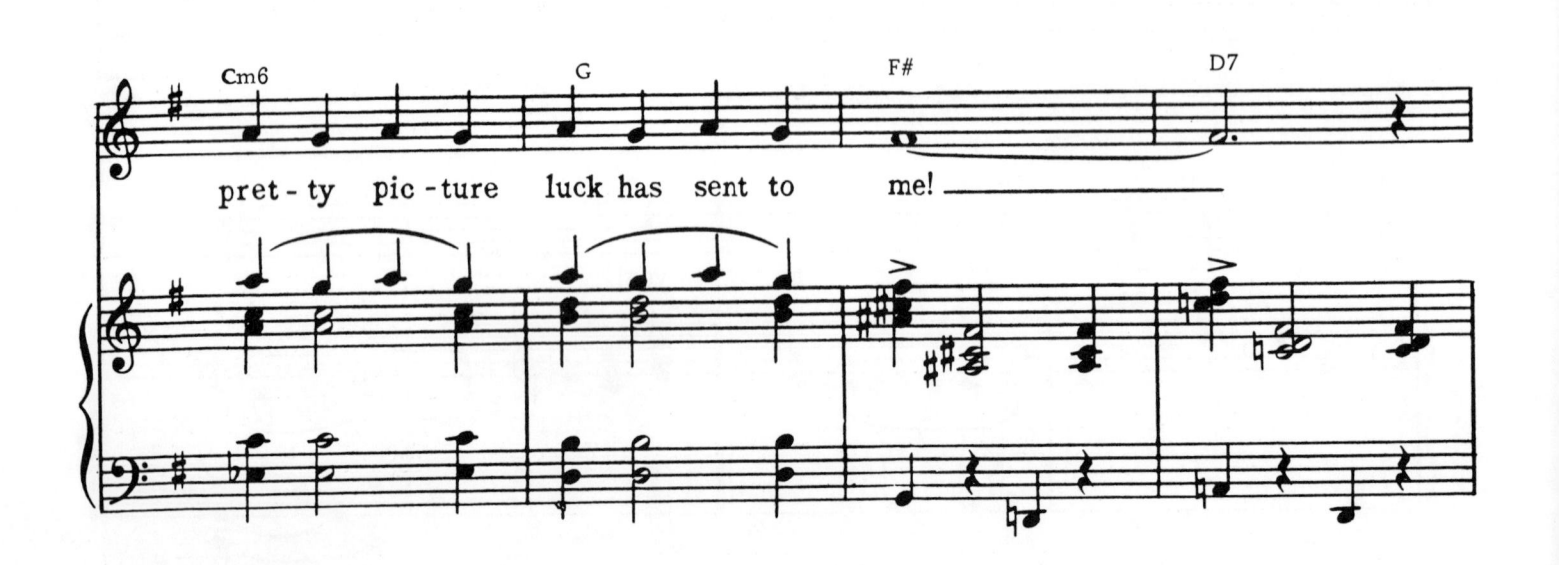

Look in-to the pu-pils of my eyes and you will see what a pret-ty pic-ture luck has sent to me!

Copyright © 1940 by Chappell & Co., Inc.
Copyright Renewed

Now my life's be-gin-ning as I bathe in your re-flect-ion Thank you luck, for guid-ing me in the right di-rect-ion!

**Refrain** (*slowly, with expression*)

Who are you to give this world of mine A light and bright-er shine?

I won - der who are you _____ to make a va - cant room A place where flow - ers bloom, And tell me who am I _____ that when I think of your face I dance in-to space so hap-py and grace-ful too_____ If that's what you can do_____ I won-der who are you?_____ you?_____

# FALLING IN LOVE WITH LOVE

Lyrics by LORENZ HART

Music by RICHARD RODGERS

Falling in love with love Is falling for make believe. Falling in love with love Is playing the fool; Caring too much is such a juvenile fancy.

Copyright © 1938 by Chappell & Co., Inc.
Copyright Renewed

D7
Gdim7
Gm
Cm
C7
Learn - ing to trust is just For chil - dren in
cresc.
Cm7
F7
Bb
Bbmaj7
school.
I fell in love with
dim.
p
Bb6
Bb
F7sus.4
F7
Cm7
F7
love one night When the moon was full,
F7sus.4
F7
F7sus.4
F7
Bbmaj7
Bb6
I was un - wise with eyes Un - a - ble to see.

Bbmaj7 Bb6 Bbmaj7 Bb6 Bbmaj7 Bb6
I fell in love with love, With love ev-er-
D7sus.4 D7 Gmaj7 G7 Cm Ddim7
last - ing, But love fell
cresc.
1.
Cm7 F7 Bb F7
out with me.
f
2.
Bb Bb6
me.
mf
f

# FROM ANOTHER WORLD

Lyrics by LORENZ HART

Music by RICHARD RODGERS

*Sandy:* Are you sure you love this guy? *Minnie:* Oh, yes! Oh, yes!

*Zacky:* That girl can feel, She could play Camille.

Copyright © 1940 by Chappell & Co., Inc.

*Sandy:* Did you smile as he passed by? *Minnie:* Not at all! Not at all!

*Sandy:* Were you that dumb? *Zacky:* She loves the bum!

Refrain

*Minnie:* You are from an-oth-er world, oh, so strange-ly

sweet,_____ When you left this other world_____ Did you guess we were destined to meet?_____ Now I hear an-oth-er song,_____ Mu-sic found in the sound of your feet,_____ You are from an-oth-er world,_____ Mak-ing mine_____ com-plete. plete._____

# EV'RY SUNDAY AFTERNOON

*Lyrics by LORENZ HART*        *Music by RICHARD RODGERS*

He: I love to do my work, Nev-er com-plain, Nev-er get tired, Don't mind the strain,
She: I work my life a-way, Think-ing of play, What will I wear? What will you say?

Copyright © 1940 by Chappell & Co., Inc.
Copyright Renewed.

I al-ways say, Old man, Wait till you're through,
Then I re-mind my-self, Old girl, you're strong,

Sun-day will come, Thurs-day comes too,
And you're in love. Life can't go wrong,

In those two days Think what you'll do,
Smile your old smile, Sing your old song.

For they're the love-ly days with you.
Wait till those dear days come a-long.

**Refrain**

*Guitar tacet* — *p-mf smoothly and not fast*

Ev-'ry Sun-day af-ter-noon and Thurs-day night ____ We'll be free as birds in flight. ____ If on Sun-day af-ter-noon We ev-er fight ____ We'll make up on Thurs-day night. ____

Leave the dish-es ____
I'm your slave, dear, ____

96

Dry your hands,_____ Change your wish-es_____
But it's bliss,_____ If you shave, dear,_____
To com-mands._____ Ev-'ry Sun-day af-ter-noon We'll be po-
We can kiss._____
lite, But we'll make love on Thurs-day night! Ev-'ry night!_____

# IT NEVER ENTERED MY MIND

*Lyrics by LORENZ HART*  *Music by RICHARD RODGERS*

I don't care if there's powder on my nose, I don't care if my hair-do is in place. I've lost the very meaning of repose, I never put a mud pack on my face. Oh, who'd have thought that I'd

Copyright © 1940 by Chappell & Co., Inc.
Copyright Renewed.

walk in a daze now, I nev-er go to shows at night, But just to ma-tin-ees now. I see the show and home I go.

**Refrain** *slowly, with warm expression*

Once I laughed when I heard you say-ing That I'd be play-ing sol-i-taire,— Un-eas-y in my eas-y chair.—

It nev-er en-tered my mind. Once you told me I was mis-tak-en That I'd a-wak-en with the sun And or-der or-ange juice for one, It nev-er en-tered my mind. You have what I lack my-self

And now I even have to scratch my back myself. Once you warned me That if you scorned me, I'd sing the maiden's pray'r again. And wish that you were there again To get into my hair again, It never entered my mind.

# WHEN YOU'RE DANCING THE WALTZ

Lyrics by LORENZ HART
Music by RICHARD RODGERS

When you're danc-ing the waltz, _____ You must not lose your head {Sir, Ma'am} _____ When you're danc-ing the waltz, _____ Lose your shy-ness in-stead, {Sir, Ma'am} _____ You are both vis-a-vis, _____ Let your fin-gers en-twine, _____ You've no need for a

Copyright © 1936 by Chappell & Co., Inc.
Copyright Renewed

102

sec - on' glass of wine.____ Sway - ing,____

Then it's one, two, three glide,____ Let your ret - i - cence

go {Sir, / Ma'am,}____ Let {his / my} arm be {my / your} guide.____

Not too close-ly, oh no, {Sir, / Ma'am,}____ For the dance of the

D7 sus4 D7 Am A♭+
mf
day Is ex - cit - ing and gay,
mf
C G Am7 D7 sus4 D7
p
You'll be car - ried a - way, When you're danc - ing the
p
1. G Bm D7
mf Guitar tacet
waltz. When you're danc - ing the
mf
2. G Gmaj7 G G
waltz.
f L.H.

# BEWITCHED

*Lyrics by* LORENZ HART

*Music by* RICHARD RODGERS

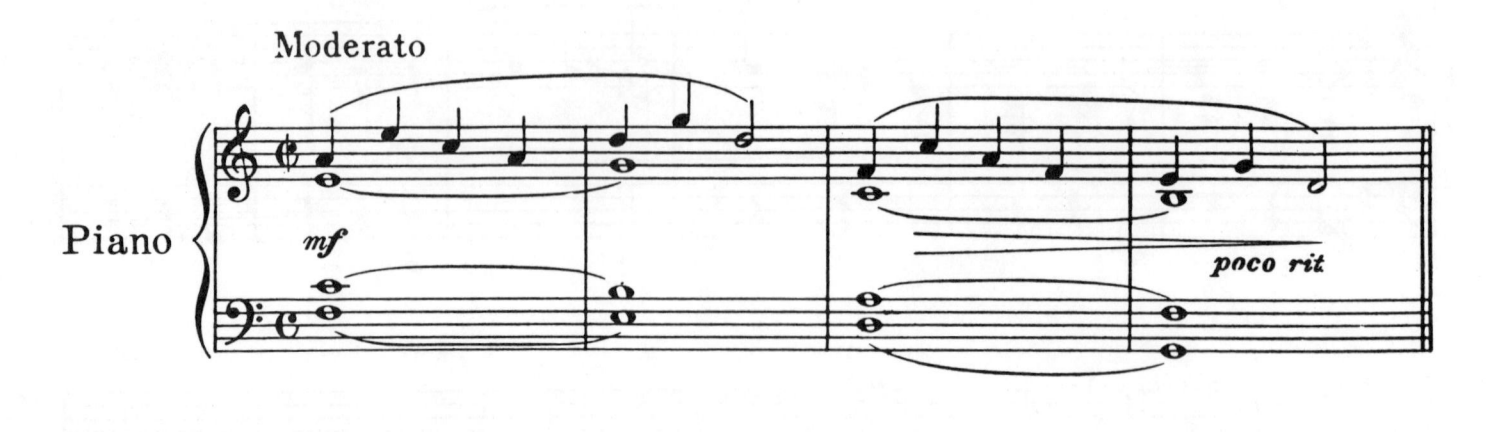

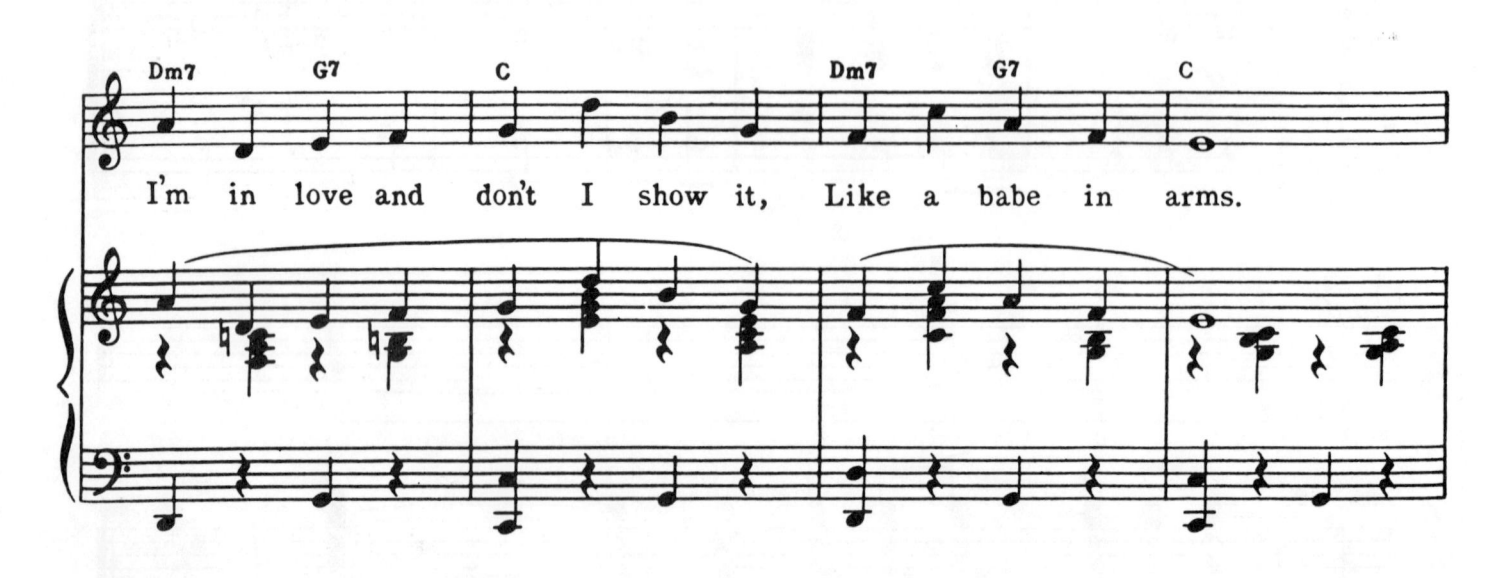

He's a fool and don't I know it, But a fool can have his charms;
I'm in love and don't I show it, Like a babe in arms.

Copyright © 1941 by Chappell & Co., Inc.
Copyright Renewed

Love's the same old sad sen-sa-tion, Late-ly I've not slept a wink,

Since this half-pint im-i-ta-tion, Put me on the blink.

**Refrain** *(slowly)*
I'm wild a-gain, Be-guiled a-gain, A sim-per-ing, whim-per-ing child a-gain, Be-witched, both-ered and be-wild-ered am

Dm G7 C G7
I. Could-n't sleep, And would-n't sleep, When
C C+ F G#dim C D7
love came and told me I should-n't sleep, Be-witched, both-ered and be-
G7 C7 F A7
wild-ered am I.
A7 Am
Lost my heart, but what of it? He is cold I a-
mp

gree, He can laugh, but I love it,— Al-though the laugh's on me. I'll sing to him, Each spring to him, And long for the day when I'll cling to him, Be-witched, both-ered and be-wild-ered am I._____ I'm I._____

# I COULD WRITE A BOOK

*Lyrics by* LORENZ HART  
*Music by* RICHARD RODGERS

A B C D E F G I never learned to spell, at least not well. One, two, three, four, five, six, seven, I never learned to count a great amount.

Copyright © 1940 by Chappell & Co., Inc.  
Copyright Renewed

But my bus-y mind is burn-ing to use what learn-ing I've got,

I won't waste an-y time, I'll strike while the i-ron is hot.

**Refrain** *(slowly, with expression)*
If they asked me I could write a book,—

— A-bout the way you walk and whis-per and

look, _____ I could write a pre-face ___ on how we met, so the world would nev-er ____ for-get, _____ And the sim-ple se-cret of the plot _____ is just to tell them that I

C C♯dim Dm7 G7 F G7
love you a lot, Then the
più espress.
C A♭7 Dm7 G7 Gm7 C7
world dis - cov - ers as my book
F Dm C G+ Dm7 G7
ends, How to make two lov - ers of
1. C Dm7 G7 2. C F C
friends. If they friends.
mf
mf

# ALL DRESSED UP (SPIC AND SPANISH)

Lyrics by LORENZ HART

Music by RICHARD RODGERS

All dressed up spic and Span-ish, But I got no place to go. Got some things I got to show, oh! All dressed up slick and Span-ish. No one takes me for a ride, Have-n't got a thing to hide. I want to go a-way Where the men make

Copyright © 1939 by Chappell & Co., Inc.
Copyright Renewed

music, And play till the night is day; Cock a doo-dle dad-dy, spic and span, spic and Span-ish, Not the type to cook or sew,— Here's the girl, but where's the beau?— I want to go a-way, a-way! way!

# YOU MUSTN'T KICK IT AROUND

Lyrics by LORENZ HART  
Music by RICHARD RODGERS

If my heart gets in your hair,— You mus-n't kick it a-round— If you're bored with this af-fair— You mus-n't kick it a-round,— Ev-en though I'm mild and meek,— When we have a brawl. If I turn the oth-er cheek—

Copyright © 1940 by Chappell & Co., Inc.  
Copyright Renewed

A7 D7 G
You mus - n't kick it at all. When I try to
Gm D7 G Dm7 G7
ring the bell, You nev - er care for the sound, The
C Cm D7
next guy may not do as well, You mus - n't kick it a -
1. G D7 2. G Am7 G
round. round.
cresc.
mf
p
f

# DO IT THE HARD WAY

*Lyrics by LORENZ HART*

*Music by RICHARD RODGERS*

Do it the hard way, And it's eas-y sail-ing,

Do it the hard way and it's hard to lose,

On-ly the soft way has a chance of fail-ing,

You have to choose,

Copyright © 1940 by Chappell & Co., Inc.
Copyright Renewed

117

# SIMPATICA

*Lyrics by LORENZ HART*

*Music by RICHARD RODGERS*

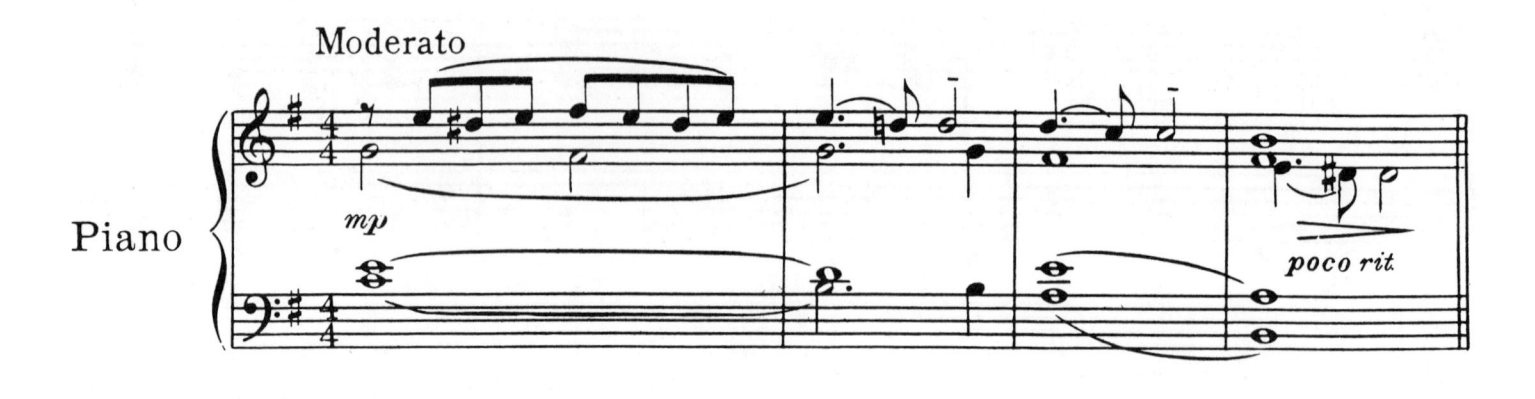

I don't des-cribe you when I say, You have im-mor-tal beau-ty.

Or when I say that you are wise, Or you're a slave to du-ty.

Copyright © 1941 by Chappell & Co., Inc.
Copyright Renewed

But you mean more to me, Than an-y-one be-fore, by far, You are

**Refrain** (*slowly with warm expression*)
Sim - pat - i - ca, One look in your eyes and I know you, Touch-ing your hand, bound me to you. You un-der-stand, For you are Sim - pat - i - ca,

D7 G D7 G D G D7 G6
Sim - pat - i - ca, You don't have to talk
D7 G D7 G6 D7 Gsus4 D7 G E dim
to in - spire me, Don't have to say you de - sire me, Day af - ter day,
D7 C D7 G C D7
You are so Sim - pat - i - ca. You speak and it's the
mf
G A B♮7 Em G7 C D7
sweet - est mu - sic I have ev - er heard, You taught me how to

G A7 D D7 G D G D7
live a-gain the day you taught me That sin-gle word: Sim-pat-i-ca. I
G6 D7 G D7 G6 D7 Gsus4 D7
know that our love must be death-less, One lit-tle kiss leaves me breath-less,
G E dim D7 C D7 G G D7
You must know this if you are Sim-pat-i-ca, And you are so Sim-
1. G Am7 D7 2. G
pat-i-ca. Sim- -pat-i-ca.
p
mf
mf

# WAIT TILL YOU SEE HER

*Lyrics by LORENZ HART*

*Music by RICHARD RODGERS*

Wait till you see her, see how she looks, Wait till you hear her laugh. Painters of paintings, writers of books, Never could tell the half. Wait till you feel the warmth of her glance,

Copyright © 1942 by Chappell & Co., Inc.
Copyright Renewed

Cmi.7 G7+(♭9) C9(5♭) C9 Fmi.7 B♭7
Pen - sive and sweet and wise. All of it love - ly,
mp
Cmi. Gmi. C9 F7 (sus.6) Fmi.
All of it thrill - ing; I'll nev - er be will - ing to free
cresc.
mf
G7 E♭mi. F7 E7 E♭7 Fmi.7
her, When you see her, You won't be -
rit.
B♭7 (sus.6) B♭7 1.E♭ 2. E♭
lieve your eyes. eyes.
a tempo
rall.
Ped.
*

# EV'RYTHING I'VE GOT

Lyrics by LORENZ HART
Music by RICHARD RODGERS

Don't stamp your foot at me, That's im-po-lite, To stamp your foot at me, Is not quite right.

Copyright © 1942 by Chappell & Co., Inc.
Copyright Renewed

All I dis-cov-er is, You're not so fine, I fear my lov-er is a swine.

**Refrain** *(brightly)*

I have eyes for you to give you dir-ty looks, I have words that do not come from chil-dren's books, There's a trick with a knife, I'm learn-ing to do, _____ And ev-'ry-thing I've got be-longs to you. _____ I've a pow'r-ful an-aes-thes-ia in my fist, _____ And the per-fect wrist to give your neck a twist, _____ There are ham-mer-lock holds

I've mas-tered a few, And ev-'ry-thing I've got be-longs to you. Share for share, Share a-like, You get struck each time I strike, You for me, Me for you, I'll give you plen-ty of noth-ing, I'm not yours for bet-ter but for worse,

And I've learned to give the well-known witches curse I've a terrible tongue, A temper for two, And ev'ry-thing I've got belongs to you. I have you.